Read & Respo

C000231324

FOR KS2

Holes

Guided reading

Shared reading

Plot, character and setting

Talk about it

Get writing

Assessment

Read & Respond

FOR KS2

Author: Liz Broad

Development Editor: Simret Brar

Editor: Vicky Butt

Assistant Editor: Rachel Mackinnon

Series Designer: Anna Oliwa

Designer: Q2A Media

Text © 2008 Liz Broad © 2008 Scholastic Ltd

Designed using Adobe InDesign

Published by Scholastic Ltd, Villiers House,
Clarendon Avenue, Leamington Spa,
Warwickshire CV32 5PR

www.scholastic.co.uk

Printed by Bell & Bain

1 2 3 4 5 6 7 8 9   8 9 0 1 2 3 4 5 6 7

British Library Cataloguing-in-Publication Data
A catalogue record for this book is available from the British
Library.

ISBN 978-1407-10001-2

Acknowledgements

The publishers gratefully acknowledge permission to reproduce
the following copyright material: **Bloomsbury Publishing plc** for
the use of extracts and the cover of *Holes* by Louis Sachar Text
© 1998, Louis Sachar (1998, Frances Foster Books an imprint
of Farrar, Straus and Giroux Inc., New York). Every effort has
been made to trace copyright holders for the works reproduced
in this book, and the publishers apologise for any inadvertent
omissions.

Holes

About the book

First published in 1998, *Holes* is a rite-of-passage novel combined with a detective story, quest and treasure hunt, written by a significant author from another culture. The structure is complex, using flashback and foreshadowing. It interweaves three separate stories which are separated by four generations and more than a hundred years, but linked through theme and symbolic action. Thus it is a text that can be used to meet many of the objectives of the PNS renewed Literacy Framework. The film of the book was released in 2003.

Stanley Yelnats is the fifth generation of his family to be affected by the curse put on his great-great-grandfather, Elya Yelnats. Elya, despondent with the sudden realisation that the girl he thought he loved was vacuous and empty-headed, forgot his bargain with the gypsy who had helped him woo her – and was subsequently cursed by her. All families have traditions, family jokes and their own special phrases, and while Stanley's parents claim not to believe in curses, it comes in handy to have a mantra when things go wrong. They can blame Stanley's no-good-dirty-rotten-pig-stealing-great-great-grandfather.

Stanley at the outset is very much a victim: overweight, bullied at school, friendless, accepting the curse of the Yelnats. His great grandfather had made a fortune on the stock market, but lost it when his stagecoach was robbed by Kissin' Kate Barlow en route from New York to California. Stanley's father is an unsuccessful inventor, filling their apartment with the smell of burning rubber as he seeks to invent a way to recycle old sneakers. Stanley is convicted of a crime he did not commit, and sentenced to 18 months at a correction camp. Naivety pervades the household: Stanley doesn't need a lawyer, he simply needs to tell the truth in court; Camp Green Lake will be like the summer camp the Yelnats have never been able to afford.

The book successfully interweaves the stories of Elya Yelnats, the inhabitants of the town of Green Lake 110 years previously and the present-day inhabitants of Camp Green Lake. It has a universal appeal, while the writing style and short chapters facilitate understanding, hooking the reader into the text.

About the author

Louis Sachar was born in 1954 in New York. Helping out at a local elementary school while at university generated many of the ideas for his first book, *Sideways Stories from Wayside School*. He qualified as a lawyer, and combined part-time legal work with writing until his books became established. Sachar's *Wayside School* series, aimed at nine- to twelve-year-olds and his *Marvin Redpost* books for younger readers, are immensely popular in the USA, making good use of his quirky sense of humour. *Small Steps*, a sequel to *Holes* which focuses on the life of Armpit after the disbanding of Camp Green Lake, was published in 2006.

> **Facts and figures**
> *Holes* has won numerous awards, including the National Book Award for Young People's Literature in 1998 and the Newbery Medal in 1999.
> The screen adaptation of *Holes* was written by Louis Sachar. The film version was released by Disney in 2003 and is available on DVD.

Guided reading

Part one: You are entering Camp Green Lake

Chapters 1–2

This opening section is designed to hook the reader straight away. It is littered with unanswered questions – a classic authorial strategy to encourage engagement with the text. What happened to the lake? What happened to the town and its people?

Discuss the choice Stanley is given at the end of Chapter 2, what do the children think he will decide? (Will he choose jail or Camp Green Lake?)

Ask the children what is unusual about Stanley's name. (It is palindromic.)

Chapter 3

Questions begin to be answered in this chapter, and the seeds of the different, interweaving stories are sown. Draw attention to the two threads: Stanley's story and that of his no-good-dirty-rotten-pig-stealing-great-great-grandfather. Create a family tree to avoid confusion:

Elya Yelnats – great-great-grandfather to Stanley
↓
Stanley Yelnats I – robbed by
Kissin' Kate Barlow
↓
Stanley Yelnats II – Stanley's grandfather
(features in the film version, not in the book)
↓
Stanley Yelnats III – father of our
hero and an inventor
↓
Stanley Yelnats IV – sent to correction camp

Discuss the fact that Elya is our hero's great-great-grandfather, but Stanley-the-Inventor's great-grandfather.

Kissin' Kate Barlow is introduced in this chapter, although her significance to the story is as yet unknown. Discuss 'outlaws' and encourage the children to consider whether they were all bad, and what might have driven them to their course of action.

Chapters 4–6

Consider how Sachar builds our knowledge of Stanley's character through inference. (Stanley considers different interpretations of the driver's parting advice to 'Be careful'.)

Point out that 'canteen' is the American word for 'water bottle'.

Can the children explain Mr. Pendanski's comment, 'You may have done some bad things, but that doesn't mean you're a bad kid' in Chapter 5?

Why does Mr. Pendanski insist on using everyone's proper names, and the boys insist on their nicknames? (Nicknames are important in terms of belonging/fellowship. Stanley feels accepted when he is dubbed 'Caveman'.) Notice the cruelty of Mr. Pendanski's attitude to Zero (Chapter 5).

Look at the reference to Barf Bag in Chapter 5. ('Lewis is still in hospital… He won't be returning.') Discuss the possibilities here and why not knowing what actually happened to Barf Bag raises tension.

Chapters 7–8

Chapter 7 is the longest to date. The structure – divided between describing Stanley's first hole and the story of Elya Yelnats – increases the sense of just how long and wearisome it was to dig that hole. What is the significance of Stanley declining a ride back to the camp? (Inner toughness; character development.)

Chapter 8 is a short, but significant, tension-raising chapter. Do the children make the connection between the diets of the yellow-spotted lizard and Mr. Sir? (Sunflower seeds.)

Chapters 9–12

Draw attention to the alteration of 'Rec(reation) Room' to 'Wreck Room'. Why might the boys

Guided reading

break everything in a room that is designed for their recreation? Discuss how punishment can affect people (make them contrite, angry, resigned…). What do the children think is the most effective way to correct people?

Ask the children to consider the definition of 'interesting' in this section. Stanley's fossil does not qualify as 'interesting'. How does he feel about this? (A clearer explanation of the term would not raise such false hopes.)

Stanley begins to realise that bullies are cowards. Derrick Dunne would have been scared of the boys at Camp Green Lake.

How effective is Mr. Pendanski as camp counsellor? (Consider his use of platitudes, attitude to Zero, element of fantasy when discussing the boys' choice of career.)

Chapter 13

Stanley finds the metal tube and gives it to X-Ray, with the suggestion that the 'discovery' is saved until the following day. This continues Stanley's acceptance into the gang. Stanley is becoming less naïve. Discuss 'rite of passage' novels and Stanley's journey to greater self-awareness and understanding of his family history.

Chapters 14–18

Focus on how Sachar increases the reader's fear of the Warden: a character rarely seen but surrounded by rumour; she knows all the boys' nicknames; her treatment of Mr. Pendanski.

More emerges about Zero: he didn't watch *Sesame Street;* can't read; has no-one to write to; he thought Stanley was his friend but can't persuade him to teach him. How is Sachar positioning the reader? (Eliciting sympathy and curiosity.)

Chapters 19–22

Focus on the interactions between the different characters. Consider the encounter with the Warden. Is her reaction what the children would expect? Why is she punishing Mr. Sir and not Stanley? Who has dug Stanley's hole in his

absence? How do you know?

What do we learn about Zero's aptitude when Stanley starts teaching him? ('I'm not stupid…')

Detective stories are like jigsaw puzzles – lots of clues that eventually fit together to reveal the truth. The final sentences of Chapter 22 provide another piece of the puzzle – or possibly two. Could the lipstick cover have belonged to Kissin' Kate Barlow?

Chapters 23–26

This section comprises a flashback to the Kissin' Kate Barlow story. Note the change in the style of writing: it becomes more descriptive, featuring more adjectives and longer sentences. The theme of smelly feet appears again and Sam the onion seller is introduced. Discuss how the Green Lake townsfolk took no chances – they used both conventional and folk medicine. Were they wise to do that? There are parallels that can be drawn between Zero and Sam: both are intelligent but uneducated. Explain the problems associated with a white woman and a black man falling in love 100 years ago.

Note how quickly 'we value education here in Green Lake' (Chapter 25) becomes burning school books because of the teacher's illicit kiss with Sam.

At the end of the Chapter 26, Sachar directs a question at the reader: 'Whom did God punish?' Use this as the basis for a class discussion.

Questions surrounding the absence of a lake at Green Lake are answered at this point.

Chapters 27–28

Zero is revealed to be Hector Zeroni. The threads between the two families are being tied together. (Madame Zeroni and Elya Yelnats.)

In Chapter 28, at the end of part one, Kissin' Kate Barlow dies and with her dies the secret of where she has buried the treasure. She prophesies that Trout Walker and his descendants will be digging for the next hundred years. Can the children make connections with the present-day story?

Guided reading

Part two: The last hole

Chapters 29–36

The change in the weather emphasises both the characters' emotions and plot details. God's thumb is revealed because of the unusual meteorological conditions. Invite the children to speculate about the shape of the rock. The change in the weather also presages the change in Zero's behaviour and his running away moves the plot forward.

Discuss how easy it is to misjudge people in the way Mr. Pendanski does Zero. Do the children think it is more character-building to teach Zero to read than to dig holes?

Examine how tension is raised as Stanley sets off to look for Zero. (Canteen empty from outset, sees his first set of lizards, odds of survival emphasised.)

In Chapter 34 a mirage is mentioned. The children could research this phenomenon.

How realistic is the finding of the boat the *Mary Lou*?

What is the purpose of *sploosh*? (Connects Zero and Stanley with the earlier story; raises links in reader's mind.)

Zero and Stanley speculate about who Mary Lou was – but the reader is already knows. Why does Sachar do this? (Gives the reader a sense of superiority.)

Chapters 37–42

Can the children identify how these chapters on the mountain combine some of the story's puzzle pieces and link the three plot strands through character actions and themes? (The finding of water and carrying of Zero mirrors the Elya story; onions link them to the story of Sam and Kate; Zero and Stanley are linked via the sneakers.)

We also learn a great deal about Zero's childhood. Ask the children to pick out aspects of Zero's upbringing. (Family stole, didn't know it was wrong, did not go to school.) How might they describe it? (Bleak, unconventional.) Does

this explain why Zero keeps himself to himself?

Chapter 42 concludes with an authorial device. Stanley asks a question which is not answered – the reader must supply the answer unaided.

Chapters 43–47

The distance that Zero and Stanley walk back to camp is emphasised (as in Chapter 7 and the digging of the first hole) by interspersing the description of the walk with revelations about Zero's childhood.

Draw attention to Sachar's use of cliffhangers to finish Chapters 44, 45 and 47: as an authorial device to keep the reader engrossed.

In Chapter 46, as the camp staff wait for Zero and Stanley to die, they tell Stanley that he was to be released the previous day – his lawyer had been to visit. Discuss the irony of the situation.

Chapters 48–49

Ask the children to complete another part of the puzzle – the link between the Warden and the Kissin' Kate Barlow story. (Her surname is Walker; Kate died prophesying Trout's descendants would be digging for treasure for many years to come.)

Discuss the lawyer – a decisive, proactive woman who moves the story swiftly on.

What is the purpose of Chapter 49? (The anecdote about Sam and the onion juice that staved off lizards, allows the reader to make connections between this and the fact that the two boys were not bitten.) Rain starts to fall. What is the symbolism of this?

Part three: Filling in the holes

Chapter 50 fills in some of the detail, but again leaves the reader to 'fill in the holes'. Why is the ending so satisfying? (Threads tied together; story came full circle when Stanley carried Zero up the hill and broke the gypsy curse; themes neatly integrated; but not all questions answered – some left to reader to infer.)

Shared reading

Extract 1

● Complete this activity after 'Does it grab you?' in Section 5.
● Read Extract 1. Tell the children that Sachar is using a classic strategy to 'hook the reader': raising questions. Model how this works, for example: *Why is it called 'Camp Green Lake' if there is no lake?* Ask the children to work in pairs to identify further questions and annotate their copy of the extract. Share and consider possible answers.
● Display an enlarged copy of the extract with questions underlined and leave sticky notes freely available. As they read on, encourage the children to speculate about possible answers, based on their reading, and to post these on the display. Include page references and their reasoning. Ideas will alter as facts are revealed, demonstrating the author's skill and highlighting narrative structure.
● Look at the structure of the sentences. Underline simple, compound and complex sentences in different colours. What do the children notice? (The majority are simple.) What is the effect? (The prose pulls no punches; menacing tone; echoes harshness of landscape.)

Extract 2

● Read Extract 2. Again, highlight the shortness of the sentences. Are there any adjectives or adverbs? Why does Sachar writelike this? (Unemotional description; treats the reader as mature, capable of drawing own conclusions.)
● How might each character be feeling? Change 'said' to reflect this. Does this improve the writing? (No – such changes emphasise the 'saying' phrase unnecessarily.)
● What do the children think of the methods of Myra and her father to facilitate choice? (Storybook characters rather than real life; defines characters through humour.)
● What adjectives can they use to describe Myra and her father?
● Underline 'Elya said nothing'. Why did he do this? Why didn't Elya pick a number? (He realises that Madame Zeroni is right about Myra.) How does Elya feel? What does this tell the reader about him?
● What will Elya do next? Why? (He will go to America; Madame Zeroni was astute about Myra so her advice must be worth following; unrequited love signals a new beginning.)
● Ask the children to write a possible next sentence for the extract.

Extract 3

● Read Extract 3. What effect does the juxtaposition of the first two lines have? Read it in a range of ways to maximise the impact.
● What do the children notice about the style of writing in the rest of the extract? (Longer sentences; descriptive; similar to the style of writing in the Kissin' Kate Barlow story.) Why might this be the case? (The start of Part two; two strands of the story merging; story moving on and possible upturn in Stanley's fortune.)
● Identify adjectives, adverbs and figurative language and explore alternatives.
● What is the significance of the last line and why is it written in italics? (It comes from Stanley's great-grandfather's story; to emphasise the link between God's thumb and the mountain Stanley has just seen.)
● Identify the symbolism in this section: God's thumb (thumb's up, scene of rescue for both Stanley and his great-grandfather); lightning (flash of understanding – moving the story forward); storm brewing (weather mirroring plot/pathetic fallacy – Zero is about to lose his temper).

Extract 1

Chapter 1

There is no lake at Camp Green Lake. There once was a very large lake here, the largest lake in Texas. That was over a hundred years ago. Now it is just a dry, flat wasteland.

There used to be a town of Green Lake as well. The town shriveled and dried up along with the lake, and the people who lived there.

During the summer the daytime temperature hovers around ninety-five degrees in the shade—if you can find any shade. There's not much shade in a big dry lake.

The only trees are two old oaks on the eastern edge of the "lake". A hammock is stretched between the two trees, and a log cabin stands behind that.

The campers are forbidden to lie in the hammock. It belongs to the Warden. The Warden owns the shade.

Out on the lake, rattlesnakes and scorpions find shade under rocks and in the holes dug by the campers.

Here's a good rule to remember about rattlesnakes and scorpions: If you don't bother them, they won't bother you.

Usually.

Being bitten by a scorpion or even a rattlesnake is not the worst thing that can happen to you. You won't die.

Usually.

Sometimes a camper will try to be bitten by a scorpion, or even a small rattlesnake. Then he will get to spend a day or two recovering in his tent, instead of having to dig a hole out on the lake.

But you don't want to be bitten by a yellow-spotted lizard. That's the worst thing that can happen to you. You will die a slow and painful death.

Always.

If you get bitten by a yellow-spotted lizard, you might as well go into the shade of the oak trees and lie in the hammock.

There is nothing anyone can do to you anymore.

Text © 1998, Louis Sachar.

Extract 2

from Chapter 7

Myra's father got down on his hands and knees and closely examined each pig, tail to snout.

"Those are two of the finest pigs I have ever seen,' he said at last. 'How am I to decide? I have only one daughter."

"Why not let Myra decide?" suggested Elya.

"That's preposterous!" exclaimed Igor, expelling saliva as he spoke.

"Myra is just an empty-headed girl," said her father. "How can she possibly decide, when I, her father, can't?"

"She knows how she feels in her heart," said Elya.

Myra's father rubbed his chin. Then he laughed and said, "Why not?" He slapped Elya on the back. "It doesn't matter to me. A pig is a pig."

He summoned his daughter.

Elya blushed when Myra entered the room. "Good afternoon, Myra," he said.

She looked at him. "You're Elya, right?" she asked.

"Myra," said her father. "Elya and Igor have each offered a pig for your hand in marriage. It doesn't matter to me. A pig is a pig. So I will let you make the choice. Whom do you wish to marry?"

Myra looked confused. "You want *me* to decide?"

"That's right, my blossom," said her father.

"Gee, I don't know," said Myra. "Which pig weighs more?"

"They both weigh the same," said her father.

"Golly," said Myra, "I guess I choose Elya—No, Igor. No, Elya. No, Igor. Oh, I know! I'll think of a number between one and ten. I'll marry whoever chooses the closest number. Okay, I'm ready."

"Ten," guessed Igor.

Elya said nothing.

"Elya?" said Myra. "What number do you guess?"

Elya didn't pick a number. "Marry Igor," he muttered. "You can keep my pig as a wedding present."

Text © 1998, Louis Sachar.

Extract 3

from Chapter 29

There was a change in the weather.

For the worse.

The air became unbearably humid. Stanley was drenched in sweat. Beads of moisture ran down the handle of his shovel. It was almost as if the temperature had gotten so hot that the air itself was sweating.

A loud boom of thunder echoed across the empty lake.

A storm was way off to the west, beyond the mountains. Stanley could count more than thirty seconds between the flash of lightning and the clap of thunder. That was how far away the storm was. Sound travels a great distance across a barren wasteland.

Usually, Stanley couldn't see the mountains at this time of day. The only time they were visible was just at sunup, before the air became hazy. Now, however, the sky was very dark off to the west, and every time the lightning flashed, the dark shape of the mountains would briefly appear.

"C'mon, rain!" shouted Armpit. "Blow this way!"

"Maybe it'll rain so hard it will fill up the whole lake," said Squid. "We can go swimming."

"Forty days and forty nights," said X-Ray. "Guess we better start building an ark. Get two of each animal, right?"

"Right," said Zigzag. "Two rattlesnakes. Two scorpions. Two yellow-spotted lizards."

The humidity, or maybe the electricity in the air, had made Zigzag's head even more wild-looking. His frizzy blonde hair stuck almost straight out.

The horizon lit up with a huge web of lightning. In that split second Stanley thought he saw an unusual rock formation on top of one of the mountain peaks. The peak looked to him exactly like a giant fist, with the thumb sticking straight up.

Then it was gone.

And Stanley wasn't sure whether he'd seen it or not.

"I found refuge on God's thumb."

Text © 1998, Louis Sachar.

Plot, character and setting

Character studies

> **Objective:** To deduce, infer and interpret information, events and ideas.
> **What you need:** Photocopiable page 15, copies of *Holes*; Extract 1.

What to do

● Read Extract 1. Highlight the two sentences that relate to the Warden, avoiding revealing her gender. What details of character does this reveal? Look at the previous sentence. Do the children know who has forbidden campers to lie in the hammock? Discuss the use of inference. Does this add to our knowledge of the Warden's character? Use the photocopiable sheet to model using the narrative to make inference.
● Read as far as Chapter 14. Were the children surprised to discover the Warden was female? Discuss stereotyping. Continue the character study on the photocopiable sheet.
● The main character in the book is Stanley Yelnats. What do we know about him? Stanley's reactions to events give us insights into his character, but we have to remember that characters develop during the course of the book. What do Stanley's actions tell us about his character? Use the photocopiable sheet to plot character development as the book unfolds.
● Refer to his: reaction to being the new boy (Chapter 5), initial assessment of Zero (Chapter 7), first letter home and acquisition of a nickname (Chapter 9), reaction to Mr. Pendanski's workshop (Chapter 12), reaction to his Mum's letter (Chapter 11), reaction to Zero's request for lessons (Chapter 18), realisation that Zero has helped him (Chapter 21).

> **Differentiation**
> **For older/more confident learners:** Ask pairs to plot the development of other significant characters and to report back to the class.
> **For younger/less confident learners:** Provide page references and support them while making inferential decisions.

Zero the hero

> **Objective:** To deduce, infer and interpret information, events and ideas.
> **What you need:** Photocopiable page 15, interactive whiteboard or flipchart.
> **Cross-curricular links:** PSHE.

What to do

● Build a portrait of Zero on the photocopiable sheet. Look at the four sentences from Zero's first appearance in Chapter 5. What can we infer about Mr. Pendanski as well as Zero, and their relationship with each other from these sentences? Do the children think Mr. Pendanski is a good camp counsellor? Draw attention to the theme of 'Zero' and 'nothing'.
● Read Chapter 12 from 'Even you, Zero'. This section confirms Mr. Pendanski's view of Zero. Why might Zero respond as he does?
● Read the passage about Zero towards the end of Chapter 7. Ask the children why this extract develops our understanding of Zero.
● Read the end of Chapter 9. Why might Zero be angry? Are the children surprised by his question? (It's the first time he has spoken.) What do we learn about Zero from the exchanges at the ends of Chapters 16 and 18? Why is Louis Sachar building up the picture like this?
● Read Chapter 22. Is Zero stupid? How does this reflect on Mr. Pendanski?

> **Differentiation**
> **For older/more confident learners:** Write a conversation between Mr. Pendanski and Mr. Sir about Zero which reveals Mr. Pendanski's attitude.
> **For younger/less confident learners:** Support the children while making the connections between actions and character.

Plot, character and setting

Yellow-spotted lizards

> **Objective:** To evaluate writers' purposes and viewpoints, and the overall effect of the text on the reader.
> **What you need:** Copies of *Holes*, access to the internet, rulers with inches.

What to do
● Read Chapter 8. Ask the children to sketch their version of the yellow-spotted lizard, actual size. Compare their sketches with each other and the front cover of the book. Does the lizard necessarily have to be green? Discuss artistic licence and discrepancies between representations.
● How does Louis Sachar build the tension here? Ask the children to list examples of the different narrative devices: description (unusual colours to body parts); direct address to reader ('a lot of people don't believe… but if one bites you…'); facts ('spots are hard to see', 'live in holes'); timing (Stanley has just dug his first hole and we know Mr. Sir has recently taken to eating sunflower seeds); vocabulary ('leaps') introduces a potential element of surprise.
● What do they think might happen? (Plot will probably involve sunflower seeds, holes and yellow-spotted lizards – and Stanley, because he is the central character.)
● Do yellow-spotted lizards, such as the ones in this book, exist? (No. They are Sachar's creation.) In pairs, ask the children to invent a creature that might pose a hazard to them in their school. Its characteristics and preferred diet and so on should relate to the school environment.

> **Differentiation**
> **For older/more confident learners:** Using similar narrative devices to those discussed above, write a chapter involving the life of their school and the fictitious creature invented above.
> **For younger/less confident learners:** Create a poster warning of the dangers of yellow-spotted lizards based on description in text.

Jigsaw puzzle

> **Objective:** To identify and comment on the structure and organisation of texts.
> **What you need:** Photocopiable page 16, copies of *Holes*, sheets of sugar paper, glue sticks, scissors.

What to do
● Discuss the fact that there are three separate stories in *Holes*: those of Elya Yelnats, Kissin' Kate Barlow and Stanley Yelnats IV. Ask the children to identify some of the major events of each strand. Louis Sachar cleverly intertwines them, gradually revealing the links between them as the book unfolds.
● Look at the photocopiable sheet. Ask groups to cut out the events and sort them into the three stories. (The final box should lead to discussion about whether it belongs to Elya or Stanley. Both characters do and don't have luck – Elya does not make his fortune, but he does marry a loyal wife; Stanley's luck changes in the end.)
● Are there any major episodes missing that the children would like to include? Allow them to write these down in a similar style of précis.
● Set out the boxes, in order, as three horizontal narrative strings and glue them in place. Ensure there is fairly wide spacing between the three strings. Keep these for the next activity.

> **Differentiation**
> **For older/more confident learners:** Identify episodes that do not fit into the three strands above (such as Chapter 40: Sam cures Becca). What purpose do these episodes serve?
> **For younger/less confident learners:** Provide additional support and discussion to facilitate separating out storylines and sequencing.

Plot, character and setting

Peaches and smelly feet

> **Objective:** To understand underlying themes, causes and points of view.
> **What you need:** Photocopiable page 17, copies of *Holes*, chart produced in the 'Jigsaw puzzle' activity, scissors, tape, glue.

What to do
- The different story strands all cover similar themes, actions and character traits. Through whole-class discussion and using the photocopiable sheet, discuss which themes, actions and traits are present in the three story strands by placing a tick in the relevant boxes.
- Provide pairs or groups with a photocopiable sheet and ask them to find evidence in the text and to note the relevant page numbers.
- Allocate a theme to a pair or group and ask them to write their own brief summary of that part of the plot.

- Ask the groups to read out their précis. Discuss their summaries, have they managed to retain all the important information, while at the same time summarising it?
- Remind the children of their narrative strands from the 'Jigsaw puzzle' activity. Together, add a neat copy of their summaries in the appropriate places. This forms a visual basis for further discussion of how Sachar interweaves the plots and themes. The page numbers provide evidence that the structure is non-linear.

> **Differentiation**
> **For older/more confident learners:** Ask the children to produce a flowchart to show how the plot unfolds gradually and includes flashback and piecemeal revelation of facts.
> **For younger/less confident learners:** The précis can be produced in pictorial form, concentrating on supported guidance of the placement of each picture within the context of the narrative.

Lights, camera, action!

> **Objective:** Respond imaginatively using different strategies to engage with texts; speak competently and creatively for different purposes and audiences.
> **What you need:** Photocopiable page 18, copies of *Holes*, writing and drawing materials, access to sound bank/musical instruments.
> **Cross-curricular links:** ICT, music, art and design.

What to do
- This activity builds on work done in the PNS Y5 Narrative Unit 5 on film narrative. Revising the main principles of the unit would be beneficial. Focus particularly on: character, colour, composition, camera, setting, sound, symbol, sequence and story.
- The task is to convert a section of the text into a film sequence. It does not have to be a section of intense action – for example, it could be introducing the characteristics of the yellow-spotted lizard. Model key aspects: strong

visuals can replace many words; music creates atmosphere; the importance of camera angle.
- In groups, the children should negotiate which section they want to 'film' and outline this on the photocopiable sheet. Any dialogue, instructions to camera, music and so on can be described alongside. Allow access to computer sound banks or musical instruments.
- Ask groups to present their extract as part of an 'audition' to get the all-important job of Director. Success criteria should be agreed in advance (faithfulness to text, visual impact, likelihood to engage audience, oral persuasion) and feedback should be based on these.

> **Differentiation**
> **For older/more confident learners:** Scan images and develop a presentation for their 'audition'.
> **For younger/less confident learners:** Enlarge the photocopiable sheet to A3 for ease of use; support the transference of their ideas to paper.

Plot, character and setting

From page to screen

> **Objective:** To respond imaginatively, using different strategies to engage with text; to compare presentation of ideas in prose and on screen.
> **What you need:** Copies of *Holes* and the film version; interactive whiteboard or flipchart.

What to do
- These activities build on the work completed in the 'Lights, camera, action!' activity.
- Recap the opening sections of the book and list the main events and characters. Put these onto a basic narrative structure.
- Working in groups or pairs, ask the children to think about how the introduction, complication and beginning of the resolution might be represented in film. What is it important for the viewer to know quickly in order to understand the story, raise the tension and so on? Encourage them to discuss, debate and list conclusions.
- Watch the opening sequences of the film. Observe the following:
  - Setting – How is this conveyed? (Sun; baked earth; boys digging; repetitive song.) What does the early use of the Barf Bag incident demonstrate? (Vacancy for Stanley; desperation of boys; raises tension.) Does putting 'if you don't bother them, they won't bother you' into the mouth of Mr. Sir work? How else might it have been done? Informing viewers of yellow-spotted lizard hazard – is this effective?
  - Complication – How is this done? (Slow-motion sneakers falling through air; small vignettes advancing story from arrest to court appearance.)
  - Different story strands – use of flashback mirroring that in book.
- Discuss the faithfulness of the film to the text.

> **Differentiation**
> **For older/more confident learners:** Ask the children to consider the portrayal of Zero on screen. Track the use of camera shots, significant action (picking up of pool ball embossed with 0) and dialogue to alert the viewer to Zero's importance. Report to the rest of the class.
> **For younger/less confident learners:** Scaffold the activity by modelling note-taking while viewing and provide a segmented sheet with headings.

Filling in the holes

> **Objective:** To evaluate writers' purposes and the overall effect of the text on the reader.
> **What you need:** Copies of *Holes*, writing materials, list of questions created at outset using Extract 1.

What to do
- Revisit the questions raised when studying Extract 1. Are they all answered by the end of Chapter 49?
- Highlight any unanswered questions and ask the children if they have any new questions. Do they expect answers to all these in the last chapter?
- Read the first paragraph of Chapter 50. Do the children realise the significance and how this ties the story of Elya to Stanley IV?
- Read the remainder of the chapter. Ask the children why key characters are present for the TV viewing. (Tying together of loose ends.)
- Who is sitting behind Hector? It implies that she is his mother. Why does Sachar not spell this out for us? (Continuing the technique of expecting the reader to 'fill in the holes'.)
- In pairs, ask the children to 'fill in this hole'. How might Hector have found his mother? Examine differences in interpretation.

> **Differentiation**
> **For older/more confident learners:** In pairs, consider what might be the message for Stanley and Zero in the verse that concludes the story.
> **For younger/less confident learners:** How is Stanley's life different now from the beginning? Ask children to list those differences, with support if necessary.

SECTION
4

Character studies

Building a picture of _____

Description in text	In my mind's eye (draw your idea here)
_____	
_____	
_____	
_____	
_____	

Use this sheet to note developments as you read *Holes*. Remember the importance of evidence from the text and page numbers

What I know about…	Evidence from text	Page

Jigsaw puzzle

Cut out all the boxes below and arrange them in chronological order on a large sheet of paper in three horizontal strands.

Finds and consumes *Sploosh*.	Lived in the town of Green Lake.	**The Story of Kissin' Kate Barlow**	Convicted of crime did not commit.
Sent to Camp Green Lake.	Forgets to carry Madame Zeroni up the hill.	Robbed by Kissin' Kate Barlow.	Killed by a yellow-spotted lizard.
The Story of Elya Yelnats	Goes to America.	Makes spiced peaches.	Becomes an outlaw.
Cursed by Madame Zeroni.	Kissed Sam the onion man.	Carries friend up the hill.	**The Story of Stanley Yelnats**
Teaches at the school at Green Lake.	Trout Walker kills Sam the onion man.	Finds case stolen by Kissin' Kate Barlow.	Teaches Zero to read.
Calls son 'Stanley', the first of a long line.	Falls in love with Myra Menke.	Digs daily holes, looking for 'interesting' items.	Father's invention makes the family wealthy.
Falls in love with Sam the onion seller.	Finds treasure that makes the family wealthy.	Kills the sheriff.	Doesn't have much luck because of the gypsy curse.

Peaches and smelly feet

Identify the theme, character trait or action in each of the three story strands.

Theme/character trait/action	Elya Yelnats	Kissin' Kate Barlow	Stanley Yelnats
Peaches.			
Water uphill.			
Rain.			
Smelly feet.			
Uneducated but bright.			
Carrying up mountain sides.			
The wrong place at the wrong time.			

Lights, camera, action!

Use this page to plan your film sequence.

Section of the book you are using			
Characters			
Location			
Scene	Dialogue	Camera angles	Music or sound effects

SCHOLASTIC
www.scholastic.co.uk

Talk about it

Does it grab you?

Objective: To reflect on reading habits and
preferences.
What you need: An enlarged version of the cover of
Holes.

What to do
- Do this activity before reading the book.
- Ask: *What makes us want to read a book?*
(Known author, interesting title, intriguing front
cover, recommendation, seen the film.)
- Enthuse about *Holes* from a personal-response
perspective. Ask pairs to discuss whether the
cover of this book makes them want to read it?
Ask them to feed back to the rest of the class.
Make a list and keep it for reference later.
- Read the blurb. Does this raise questions?
Invite speculation about genre, plot, setting and
characters. List these questions.
- When the class has finished reading the book,
revisit these lists. Have the children changed
their viewpoint as a result of reading the text?
Were their expectations realised? Should one
always judge a book by its cover?
- It is important to develop the notion that it is
acceptable not to like a book – different books
appeal to different readers – but 'give a book a go'
is a worthwhile philosophy to adopt in order that
we develop a taste for a wide range of books.

Differentiation
For older/more confident learners: Ask the children
to Identify words and phrases in the blurb that have
been chosen to encourage the purchase of the text.
For younger/less confident learners: Support
children with vocabulary.

Dig it!

Objective: To use dramatic techniques, including
work in role, to explore ideas and texts.
What you need: Garden spade lengthened to five feet
by lashing a broom handle to it, chalk for marking
playground or masking tape for indoor floor, string,
ruler, roll of sugar paper/lining paper.
Cross-curricular links: Mathematics.

What to do
- Write on the board: 'You are to dig one hole
each day, including Saturdays and Sundays. Each
hole must be five feet deep, and five feet across
in every direction. Your shovel is your measuring
stick.' (Chapter 4.) Discuss how large this actually
is and estimate how long it might take to dig one
in baked earth.
- Construct the five foot shovel and mark out a
hole. Allow the children to handle the shovel and
stand in centre of the 'hole'. Ask them for words to
describe how they would feel if they were Stanley
in this situation. Extend this activity by digging
outside if possible, pointing out that it would be
dangerous to try to dig such a hole completely
without shoring up the sides.
- Draw round the outline of a child five feet
tall. Mount the outline on a display, with
the feet touching the floor. The children can
measure themselves against this to imagine
themselves at the bottom of the hole. Use this to
represent Stanley. List his feelings in the centre
of the outline and link this to a description of
incidents listed round the outside, making the
connection between events and emotions. This
activity should be ongoing during the reading of
the book.
- Read Chapter 7. Ask the children to construct
thought bubbles to add to the outline of Stanley.

Differentiation
For older/more confident learners: Encourage them
to do some problem solving of how to measure and
mark out a hole five feet in diameter.
For younger/less confident learners: Discuss the
children's perception of the size of the hole before
creating one with them.

Talk about it

Meet group D

> **Objective:** To explore, develop and sustain ideas through talk.
> **What you need:** Photocopiable page 22, copies of *Holes*.

What to do

● Give the children a copy of the photocopiable sheet and read Chapter 5. Ask them to complete the nickname column as you read. We do not find out what Zero's real name is at this point – what effect does this have? (Theme of 'nothing'; underlines Mr. Pendanski's attitude to him; another question in the reader's mind.)

● How important is it that we do not find out Zero's real name until Chapter 27? (Another piece of the jigsaw – links Stanley's story to Zero's via their ancestors.)

● Discuss nicknames. (Usually terms of endearment but not here; indication of solidarity in adversity – and that you are accepted.) Why do the boys reject the use of their real names? (Nicknames give status but also anonymity.)

● We gradually build up a picture of the inhabitants of Tent D through a range of incidents. Ask the children, in groups or pairs, to read the relevant episodes indicated on the photocopiable sheet and discuss what each incident reveals about each character. Make brief notes and feed back into whole class discussion.

> **Differentiation**
> **For older/more confident learners:** Ask the children to consider why the other characters are not explored in the same detail as Stanley and Zero. (Not critical to plot.)
> **For younger/less confident learners:** Encourage children, through discussion and group reading, to develop understanding that incident reveals character – reader has to develop inferential skills.

What are they thinking?

> **Objective:** Use dramatic techniques, including work in role, to explore ideas and texts.
> **What you need:** Copies of *Holes*, large pieces of paper, scissors, digital camera.
> **Cross-curricular links:** PSHE, ICT.

What to do

● Tell the children they are going to investigate further the characters in group D.

● Read Chapter 12. Discuss Mr. Pendanski's approach. Is he right to encourage the boys in this way? (Good to have ambition vs being realistic.) Are the boys taking the counselling session seriously? What is the evidence for this? (X-Ray's response to the idea that Magnet might be a monkey trainer.) What effect does this have on the boys' relationship with Mr. Pendanski? Invite groups to perform a freeze-frame of the scene, using body language and expression to demonstrate personality. Evaluate their efforts.

● Cut out large thought bubbles and ask some children to hold these in place above the heads of children-in-role deemed to have represented the scene well. Photograph the results (get permission before taking photographs of children). View the images and discuss what each character might be thinking. Model this process in writing.

● Ask the groups to produce similar freeze-frames for scenes involving Zero: start of Chapter 15, the end of Chapter 19 and the dramatic moment in Chapter 30. Ask them to write thoughts on thought bubbles and photograph the results. The photographs can form the basis of a display.

> **Differentiation**
> **For older/more confident learners:** Invite children to devise a dialogue between X-Ray and Magnet in the shower after the stealing of the sunflower seeds.
> **For younger/less confident learners:** Ask children to devise an oral retelling of the sunflower seed incident from Magnet's perspective.

Talk about it

But I'm innocent!

> **Objective:** To use a range of oral techniques to present engaging narratives.
> **What you need:** Photocopiable page 23.

What to do

● This activity can take place after reading Chapter 6.

● Tell the children they are going to imagine they are Stanley, telling the story of the events leading up to his conviction to an impartial listener. What do we know about Stanley so far? (Bullied; naïve; cursed.) What are the facts of the story? (Late leaving school because of Derrick Dunne; stolen sneakers fell from freeway overpass and landed on his head.) What assumptions have been made? (An unlikely story so he must be guilty.)

● Using the photocopiable sheet, model how to make notes to develop storytelling prompt cards. Ask the children to work on their own versions, noting key phrases and events. They should practise telling the story using the prompts from all the columns, then fold over and use first two columns and finally only the first column.

● Discuss the essential ingredients of storytelling: strong narrative structure; clear sequencing; use of 'signposts' ('next', 'before'); importance of eye contact, intonation, gesture and body language. Consider the use of the dramatic pause and the need to engage the listener. List success criteria.

● In pairs, the children should take turns to tell their story. Feedback with reference to the success criteria.

> **Differentiation**
> **For older/more confident learners:** Ask the children to develop the storytelling to signal Stanley's naivety, without actually saying 'I was rather naïve because I thought…'.
> **For younger/less confident learners:** Tell them to use fewer prompt cards and focus on the main events.

Conscience alley

> **Objective:** To use the techniques of dialogic talk to explore ideas, topics and issues.
> **What you need:** Photocopiable page 24, copies of *Holes*.
> **Cross-curricular links:** PSHE.

What to do

● Read from Chapter 31 ('He returned to his tent') to the end. Ask the children to consider the options open to the Warden. (Going out to look for Zero vs erasing him from the records.) Divide the class in two and place them in lines facing each other. Invite one line to think of reasons why the Warden should instigate a search, and the other line to consider reasons why the Warden should delete him from the system. Allow some thinking and paired discussion time.

● Now ask one child from each line alternately to contribute their idea. Assume the role of the Warden and listen to opposing ideas, walking down conscience alley. Summarise and make your decision in role.

● Using the photocopiable sheet, ask children to list the main arguments. Arrange the class into six groups, each responsible for one of characters on the photocopiable sheet. Using the arguments as the basis for their discussion, devise a representation to the judge at the Warden's trial.

● Rearrange the groups so there is one of each character in a group. Acting as judge, listen to representations before sentencing the Warden.

> **Differentiation**
> **For older/more confident learners:** Invite them to devise the judge's summing up at the end of the trial.
> **For younger/less confident learners:** Encourage them to listen carefully and reform ideas in their own words.

Talk about it

Meet group D

Use this sheet to make notes about the characters in the story.

Real name	Nickname
Stanley Yelnats	
	Zero

Real name	Nickname	Episode	What does this tell us?
Alan		end Ch 11	
		start Ch 19	
		Ch 30	
Rex		start Ch 7	
		mid Ch 9	
		end Ch 10	
		start Ch 11	
		end Ch 13	
		end Ch 48	
Jose		end Ch 10	
		mid Ch 19	
		end Ch 10	
Theodore		end Ch 5	
		mid Ch 9	
		end Ch 10	
		end Ch 19	
Ricky		end Ch 19	
		end Ch 17	

Talk about it

But I'm innocent!

Plan your retelling by making notes in the right-hand column. Practise the retelling: try it using the first and middle columns, then only the first column.

Introduce self	Name	
	Age	
	Where live	
	Physical attributes	
Family history	The story of Elya	
	Family curse	
	Father's inventions	
Scene in school	School bully – describe	
	Why you?	
	Incident in the restroom (smells, sounds, sights)	
Scene by underpass	Feelings carrying soggy notebook	
	Smells, sounds, sights around you	
	Raining sneakers	
	Feeling when hit	
Scene in court	Atmosphere	
	Judge – description	
	Telling the truth	
Verdict	Were you surprised?	
	Feelings at verdict	
	Description of options	
Decision	Pros and cons of jail	
	Pros and cons of camp	
	Choice	

Conscience alley

What might the Warden do when Zero disappears? List ideas below.

Look for Zero	Erase Zero from system
1. _____	1. _____
2. _____	2. _____
3. _____ WARDEN	3. _____
4. _____	4. _____
5. _____	5. _____
6. _____	6. _____
7. _____	7. _____

How might these characters react to each of the Warden's decisions? Make notes to help you plead your case.

Zero	Stanley
Zero's mum	Zero's lawyer
Mr. Pendanski	Warden's lawyer

Get writing

Very scary

> **Objective:** To vary and adapt sentence structure for meaning and effect.
> **What you need:** Flipchart or interactive whiteboard, writing materials.

What to do
- Look again at Extract 1 from 'Here's a good rule…' to 'always'. Read it out loud. Discuss the use of one-word sentences – reassure the children that it is acceptable practice. Take out the word 'usually' and re-read. What happens? (Removes tension and becomes rather reassuring.)
- Ask the children, in pairs, to make a list of synonyms for 'usually' and try inserting them. Do they work as well? Develop into a whole-class discussion.
- Write a short piece describing an ordinary, everyday event: for example, getting up in the morning, coming to school, lunchtime routines and so on. Model an opening, which should be in the present tense, for example: 'Each morning I get up at 7am'. Read a few examples – very ordinary! Now insert 'usually' (or a synonym if a good one has been found) in the same way Louis Sachar does at the end of each sentence and see what happens.
- In pairs or groups, ask children to practise reading the pieces out loud in a suitably menacing tone, with dramatic pauses to heighten effect. Perform for another class.

> **Differentiation**
> **For older/more confident learners:** Can they find a piece of music that complements their writing? Create a recording of their written piece, with appropriate musical accompaniment to heighten atmosphere.
> **For younger/less confident learners:** Use a writing frame to structure chronological writing.

Rules, rules, rules

> **Objective:** To organise ideas into a coherent structure, including layout.
> **What you need:** Copies of *Holes*, writing equipment.

What to do
- Read the sections relating to Stanley's arrival at Camp Green Lake (Chapters 4 and 5).
- Discuss the different ways rules are written – for example:
No Smoking.
Absolutely No Smoking.
Patrons are kindly asked to refrain from smoking.
Can the children think of any more variations? Which is most likely at Camp Green Lake?
- Ask the children to imagine what rules might be written by the camp officials – and the penalties. These should be consistent with the text. Rank the rules in order of importance, with appropriately scaled punishments. For example: 'Holes must be… Penalty: another hole to be dug the same day.' (Highlight the sentence construction here.)
- Look at the use of 'rule' in: 'Here's a good rule to remember…' (Chapter 1). This time 'rules' means 'knowledge'. Think about the advice that Stanley might give to the next new boy at Camp Green Lake to ensure that they fit in well, make friends – survive. Ask the children in groups to devise a 'Camp Green Lake Guide: How to Make Your Stay Successful'. This will be constructed differently from the rules above, as it will include explanations. For example: 'It's not a good idea to talk about important things in camp – the Warden is listening.'

> **Differentiation**
> **For older/more confident learners:** Ask them to change the survival guide into formal rules.'
> **For younger/less confident learners:** Encourage them to work in pairs to construct the rules, with adult support if necessary.

Get writing

Wish you were here

> **Objective:** To use and adapt a range of forms, suited to different purposes and readers.
> **What you need:** Photocopiable page 28, internet access and data projector, Stanley's letter to his parents (Chapter 9), writing materials.
> **Cross-curricular links:** ICT.

What to do

● You need to have read to at least Chapter 10 before attempting this activity.

● If possible, look at a holiday scheme website. Record as many camp activities as possible. Have any children had any experience of summer camps? Discuss the activities and what any they think they might particularly enjoy. Move towards the notion of 'trying something new' and their possible feelings before and after.

● Discuss the need to reassure parents and the contents of Stanley's letter. What will his parents want to know? (His journey there; what the accommodation is like; companions, activities and so on.) Now display the opening section of Stanley's letter to his parents and ask in what ways this is unsatisfactory. (Not enough information; needs paragraphing.)

● Use the photocopiable sheet to outline the realities of Camp Green Lake and devise alternatives appropriate for parental consumption. The right-hand column can then form the basis of each paragraph of a letter home. Model the features of a personal letter and an appropriate form of opening paragraph, ensuring that the tone is upbeat and positive. Remind the children that each paragraph will contain several sentences on each subject.

> **Differentiation**
> **For older/more confident learners:** Ask the children to investigate American summer camps and report back on the kinds of activities that are available, accommodation, cost and so on.
> **For younger/less confident learners:** Create a picture postcard of how Stanley would want his parents to envisage Camp Green Lake and write an appropriately cheerful message home.

Advertising campaign

> **Objective:** To use structural and presentational features for meaning and impact.
> **What you need:** Photocopiable page 28, writing and art materials, leaflets and prospectuses for recreational activities or places to visit.
> **Cross-curricular links:** ICT, art and design.

What to do

● Remind the children of the conditions at Camp Green Lake and reflect on the differences between a real summer camp and this correctional facility, using the photocopiable sheets completed for the 'Wish you were here' activity.

● Examine the leaflets you have collected and identify the main features. (Glossy presentation, slogans, visuals, fonts, persuasive language.)

● Use the second column of the photocopiable sheet to design a leaflet to persuade people to come to Camp Green Lake Summer Camp.

● Now look at the first column. How could these features be turned to advantage? For example, digging holes – fitness training for arm-wrestling. In pairs, encourage them to develop their ideas and design a second leaflet to advertise Camp Green Lake the correctional facility.

● Devise a checklist of persuasive features for television advertisements, based on the work above. Ask groups to write an advertisement for each camp. Use the checklist to assess them.

> **Differentiation**
> **For older/more confident learners:** Write a jingle to accompany the television advert.
> **For younger/less confident learners:** Design a poster for both types of camp.

Get writing

I did, did I?

> **Objective:** To write independently and creatively for purpose, pleasure and learning.
> **What you need:** Photocopiable page 29, writing materials, dictionaries.
> **Cross-curricular link:** Mathematics.

What to do

● Write the title of this activity on the board and ask the children to identify its special characteristic. Explain that, like Stanley Yelnats, this is a palindrome, from Greek and meaning 'running back again'. How did they feel when they first realised that Stanley's name was palindromic?

● Are there any palindromic names in the class? Which make of car becomes a palindrome if the article is included? (A Toyota.) In pairs, list as many palindromic words as they can think of – then use dictionaries to extend the list. Did they develop any strategies to help locate them (for example, thinking about possible letter combinations for word endings and trying them backwards)?

● Discuss the palindromic sentences on the photocopiable sheet. Verify accuracy of the well-known examples given. Complete the sheet.

● Through discussion, develop a strategy that might enable the children to create their own palindromic sentences. (Constructing lists of words that work backwards as well as forwards, such as was/saw, pot/top.)

● Challenge: 7th July is a palindromic date if written 7.07.07. What are other palindromic dates? Is there a pattern?

> **Differentiation**
> **For older/more confident learners:** Write a story with a palindromic punchline. Challenge them to include words that rely on each other to be palindromic, such as 'nurses run'. Palindromic sums can also be set as a challenge in numeracy.
> **For younger/less confident learners:** With support if necessary, construct palindromic sentences.

Dilemma

> **Objective:** Express subtle distinctions of meaning, by constructing sentences in varied ways.
> **What you need:** Photocopiable page 30, copies of *Holes*, writing equipment.
> **Cross-curricular link:** PSHE.

What to do

● Re-read Chapter 19, where Magnet steals Mr. Sir's sunflower seeds and Stanley is yet again in the wrong place at the wrong time.

● What would be the consequences of lying or telling the truth about this incident? Use the photocopiable sheet to explore each action.

● Discuss the issues relating to this: stealing is wrong, being loyal to friends is right – but when that friend has stolen? Should Stanley tell the truth or accept the blame? From what we know about Stanley so far, which action do the children think he is going to take?

● Being in the wrong place at the wrong time is a theme of the book. What might be going through Stanley's head as he rides in the truck to the Warden's hut? Note ideas on the photocopiable sheet and use this to write the internal dialogue Stanley is having with himself.

● Imagaine the Warden is absent when Stanley arrives and he is told to write the facts down. Ask children to produce two versions, one admitting to stealing, one telling the truth.

> **Differentiation**
> **For older/more confident learners:** Stanley has decided to tell the truth. Work in role to devise the dialogue when Stanley returns to face Group D.
> **For younger/less confident learners:** Ask them to write the version of events the children think the more likely action Stanley will take.

Cet writing

SECTION
6

Wish you were here

List what Camp Green Lake is really like under 'Reality' and how Stanley's parents would like to believe it to be under 'Myth'.

Reality	Myth

Journey

Accommodation

Food

Friends

Activities

Get writing

I did, did I?

Tick the box if these famous examples are true palindromic sentences

A man, a plan, a canal – Panama	
Able was I 'ere I saw Elba	
Madam, I'm Adam	

Can you think of a response to the last one?

Sir, I'm __ __ __ __

Now try these:

Top s__ __ __
Borrow __ __ __ __ __
No, tie __ __ __ __
Was it a car o__ __ __ __ __ __ __ __ __?
Did Hannah say __ __ __ __ __ __ __ __ __ __ __?

What strategy did you adopt?
What might be the punchline for this story? The clues are in the text.

Nayan was making his packed lunch ready for the school outing next day. He had already made the sandwiches and found the drink and chocolate biscuit. Then he remembered that their lesson on healthy eating had encouraged them to eat plenty of fruit. He went to the fridge. Bananas, apples, pears, mango… what should he take? Lemon was his favourite. He knew the journey would be long and that he might get rather thirsty, so Nayan decided to take a slice of melon too. But, when he opened the fridge door he found there was…   __ __ __ __ __ __ __ __ , __ __ __ __ __ __ __

Get writing

The truth of the matter

Action	Consequence
Magnet tells truth.	
Magnet lies.	
Stanley tells truth.	
Stanley lies.	

Stanley's thoughts as he rides in the truck.

Oh yes, he did.	Oh no, he didn't.

Assessment

Assessment advice

The activities in this *Read & Respond* are structured to facilitate ongoing assessment. Children's understanding of the text can be assessed through questioning, role play, hot-seating, engagement with and outcomes from the range of activities suggested.

Building assessment opportunities into lesson planning allows the teacher to pre-empt misunderstanding and develop the children's skills of prediction, inference and deduction – all of which contribute to a satisfying engagement by the children in the text.

Ensuring that the children understand success criteria for taught sessions encourages them to play a proactive role in their own learning. Reading a text such as *Holes* places large demands on the children's reading abilities, as it is essential that both literal and inferential reading takes place, and it is important to have a range of assessments that gauge both.

Assessment activity

> **Assessment focus:** To evaluate writers' purposes and viewpoints, and the overall effect of the text on the reader; to develop strategies to compare film and book to establish veracity to authorial intention.
>
> **What you need:** Photocopiable page 32, the film version of the book, writing materials.

What you need

● Remind the children of work done in the 'Lights, camera, action!' activity on storyboarding and on character, colour, composition, camera, setting, sound, symbol, sequence and story.

● Think about the film version and discuss what might be similar or different. Work already done in the 'From page to screen' activity will have alerted them to the fact that some aspects of the book have been changed (Stanley is not fat at the outset, order of some events changed) and the possible reasons for this. What other differences might there be? (Scenes added that are not in the book; episodes from book missing from film.) Why? (To provide additional information; not essential to understanding film.)

● Watch the film and use the photocopiable sheet to identify similarities and differences, in the storyline, character, setting and authorial intention. Both writing and ensuing discussion will clearly indicate the children's understanding of authorial intention and provide an opportunity to explore possible misconceptions, develop a wide range of opinions and summarise literal and inferential aspects of the text. In addition, the motives for change can be explored.

● Similarities will include representation of main characters, baked earth, scorching sun, modern and historical storylines, use of flashback, considerable chunks of dialogue.

● Differences will include Stanley not being fat at outset, too many trees at Camp Green Lake, three generations of Yelnats living in family apartment.

● Additional scenes will include the police visit to Stanley and his grandfather's bedroom, Mr. Pendanski's venomous 'buddy boy' when addressing Zero.

● Episodes missing from film will include Derrick Dunne's treatment of Stanley's notebook.

From page to screen

Similarities between film and book

Differences between film and book

Scenes added into film

Scenes missing from film